Can We Talk? No!

Mediate, Don't Litigate

Can We Talk? No!
Mediate, Don't Litigate

A Client's Primer to Private Voluntary Mediation

By Leo Hura, JD, Mediator
Mediate With LH, LLC
Honolulu, Hawaii

mediatewithlh@mediate.com
www.mediate.com/mediatewithlh
808-393-0687

Can We Talk? No!
Mediate, Don't Litigate

Library of Congress Control Number: 2008905997

ISBN: 978-1-59824-861-6

First Edition
Published July 2008
E-BookTime, LLC
6598 Pumpkin Road
Montgomery, AL 36108
www.e-booktime.com

Why Should You Read This Primer?

As if you don't have enough complications in life, you are involved in a dispute where direct negotiations are failing. Like most people in America, you consider hiring an attorney, filing a complaint, and going to court. However, you've heard too many horror stories about court experiences. You wish there was another way to get your opponent to continue negotiating. Maybe you want to find a way to limit your costs which would be consumed in litigation. You don't want an imposed decision. You want flexibility in crafting your own agreement. For example you and your opponent may wish to barter services as part of an agreement. Welcome to private voluntary mediation!

My name is Leo Hura and I am a mediator. I'm excited to share my knowledge about mediation as a negotiation, collaboration, and problem-solving process to help you and your opponent reach an agreement to resolve a dispute. This primer is designed to help you decide whether voluntary mediation is right for you.

I've built the discussion around dispute situations, one of which might resemble your case. In the first, I describe a dispute among neighbors, while in the second, there's a landlord-tenant dispute. I also use an unrelated car accident and family caregiver scenarios to illustrate how mediation is applied in other contexts than in our two main examples. These disputes are fictional and simplified for explanation purposes. If the dispute is important enough for you to consider voluntary mediation, it's important you read this primer.

Our Hypothetical Mediation Scenarios

Judy and John – Neighbors with Issues

Judy and John own adjoining residential properties. Up until now they have been good and understanding neighbors. Judy, a single mother, has her beloved dog "Fluffy," her Banyan tree, and two teenagers who love their music. This morning, her neighbor John is running late for work. As he rushes out the door, he hears the usual sounds of Fluffy barking, Judy's kids talking, and their friend's car stereo blaring while he waits to take the teens to school. In his hurry, John slips on something soft in his driveway. Before he can ask the kids to move their car, which is blocking his exit, he trips on a root from Judy's tree that is growing in his driveway. He falls onto his garbage container, which overturns and spills its contents onto Judy's property. Meanwhile, Fluffy has become excited. "Fluffy" is a 70-pound Boxer. She jumps the fence to say "hello." John is petrified of dogs. John runs to and ducks into his car, smacking his head on the door frame. With Fluffy up on her paws in John's window, John notices the unmistakable smell of Fluffy doo-doo and traces the smell to the bottom of his new shoes. Meanwhile, Judy, coming out of her house, sees the commotion. She runs over to John's driveway and slips on all the garbage and falls. The kids rush over to help her into the house. John and Fluffy are left to fend for themselves. Soon, police, fire, and EMS arrive. Their sirens frighten Fluffy, who runs away. Someone calls the animal control officer. Neighbors gather for a look. A very embarrassed John exits his car to answer numerous questions. Later, John rinses his shoes under his garden hose. When he finally gets back to his house, he has a black-and-blue mark on his forehead and a growing headache.

A few days later, Judy returns from the hospital with a leg cast. John has missed an equal number of work days getting an MRI and recovering from the pain in his head. When Judy arrives, John steps outside and they exchange smiles. Then Judy begins to cry and disappears into her house. John had tried to call her in the hospital, but was told she was receiving "no visitors." There are no signs of Fluffy. When Judy was in the hospital, the teens partied into the night. As John left the house for work, the kids and their friends gave John increasingly dirty looks. His car has been vandalized and is now sporting a number of long scratches on his car finish.

John takes stock of his situation and options. He doesn't want to move. He's sure Judy will also stay. He doesn't want an adversarial relationship, tied up in litigation, potential involvement with police, or the inability to speak to his nearest neighbor. He wants to take the initiative. He wants to hear what Judy has to say and he wants to negotiate. He hears about a friend's positive experience with voluntary mediation.

He knows Judy has "issues" and so does he. Beyond insurance liability for the medical costs, he's concerned about his own rights with regards to Judy's kids, Fluffy, and the tree roots growing into his property.

Being a thorough person, John begins his review of voluntary mediation. He believes mediation could be an option for Judy and him to resolve their issues in a way which can preserve their relationship.

Mariko and Kimo – Landlord-Tenant Issues

Mariko is an owner-landlord and Kimo is her tenant. They have a one-year written lease. For the first six months, Kimo pays his rent on time, abides by the house rules, and is to all appearances a model tenant. In the seventh month, however, the rent stops with no explanation. Mariko sends an overdue notice with a note: "Let's discuss." Where previously "aloha" had been enthusiastically exchanged, sullen and averted looks become the norm. Mariko figures something extraordinary must be going on and just leaves it alone until the rent again becomes due. Again, there is no payment. When she calls Kimo's number, the message indicates the phone has been disconnected. By now, Kimo is actively avoiding Mariko. She sends another rent overdue notice to Kimo. This time, her attached note says they must talk; Mariko is covering the utilities and reminds him of the late payment penalty. She no longer sees Kimo. As the next month rolls in, she hopes against hope Kimo will pay, or at least communicate with her about the unpaid rent. However, by mid-month nothing happens. A complicating factor for Mariko is that she and Kimo work for the same company, although different offices. Kimo's father is the company's owner. Mariko and Kimo will soon be working together on a new project.

Introduction to Private Voluntary Mediation

Private voluntary mediation begins with a decision by you and your opponents to enter into mediation. Mediation is a negotiating process. A mediator will play a pivotal role in guiding you and your opponent through an "interest"-based or competitive negotiation and towards reaching an agreement with your opponent. Some additional terms used in this primer are defined below:

- "Disputants" or "opponents" are people directly involved in a dispute. They could be people having an inter-personal dispute, a business dispute, or a myriad of other types of dispute.
- "Voluntary" means that the disputants enter into mediation of their own free and mutual choice. There are no court orders making them go into the mediation process.
- "Negotiation" in the mediation context means:
  - Collaboration by opponents and problem solving to reach an agreement which is often referred to as interest based negotiation. In this primer we focus on collaborative negotiations.
  - Competitive negotiations where opponents nego-tiate competitively within fixed boundary. For example, in a landlord/tenant dispute opponents are negotiating about who pays for damages to an apartment? Each is going to negotiate to pay the least or nothing.
- "Issues" are sources of a dispute.
- "Interests" are those conditions which have to be met before a person agrees to do something. An example

of an interest might be to maintain a relationship with a person with whom the dispute has arisen.

- "Needs", if satisfied, allow disputants to move on with life or close business transactions. For example I may be demanding money to cover losses or to pay to fix the damage to my automobile or apartment.
- "Mediators" are professionals who are trained, experienced, and skilled in enabling negotiation between disputants. In other words, when direct negotiations are failing, mediators bring their skills to the table to continue or re-start negotiations. In most cases, the outcome sought from mediation is mutual agreement.

Examples of Issues, Interests, and Needs		
Example	Property Damage	Family Care
Issue	A car is damaged in an accident and must be repaired	A caregiver oversteps authority in financial matters in "care" of elderly Mom
Interest	Repair the car	Protect Mom and her estate from exploitation
Need	$'s to cover the cost to repair the car	Re-define the caregiver's responsibilities and re-assert the family's authority

How does voluntary mediation fit in with the peaceful resolution of disputes in our legal system? Where "relationships" exist, voluntary mediation fills a gap between direct negotiation and litigation. Relationships can take many forms, as for example through contracts, geographical location – as among neighbors – or through personal relationships such as marriage.

Judy and John have a neighbor-to-neighbor relationship formed by ownership and occupancy of adjacent houses. The "incident" that fateful day changed their relationship from being communicative and tolerant neighbors to two neighbors with issues. In their case the issues include:

- Liability for injuries suffered by Judy and John
- Liability for pain, suffering, and lost workdays
- A lost dog
- Trespass issues caused by the tree roots
- Judy's teenagers actions before and after Monday morning

In Mariko's and Kimo's case, the relationship is landlord/tenant gone wrong, with issues like:

- Breach of lease
- Unpaid rent
- Penalties
- Their relationship at a common workplace

For some facing John and Mariko's issues, the reaction might be: "Sue!" However, neither John nor Mariko has the court system in mind. Each wants to explore voluntary private mediation. Let's explore with them:

- How voluntary mediation fits into the American legal system
- What voluntary mediation is
- Whether John and Mariko's cases are ripe for voluntary mediation

In an ideal world, we would work with our opponents to peacefully resolve disputes. However, dispute resolution often proves difficult. As a result, over time we've established processes within our legal system to keep dispute resolutions peaceful.

In America, our justice system allows us to file legal complaints, essentially asking for arbitrators or judges to intercede, hear the evidence, and make decisions for us based on law. We can go to court on our own or we can hire attorneys to advocate our positions for us. The court system we utilize is described as "adversarial." Adversarial means that when we present our arguments to the court or arbitrator, we're trying to prove we are right and our opponent is wrong.

Mediation is different. A mediator does not deal in who is right and who is wrong. A mediator enables opponents who can no longer negotiate directly to continue negotiations as a means of reaching mutual agreement. There are a number of pathways to mediation.

Pathways to Mediation

Relationship Formed

Issues Arise

Decision

Trial or Arbitration

Direct Negotiations

Mediation

Court Ordered

Agreement

Voluntary

In a relationship when issues arise, our usual first step is to attempt direct negotiations. If communications break down, we may look for a third party, such as a mediator, to help us reach an agreement. One way to get to mediation is for you and your opponent to agree to voluntary mediation. If your opponent refuses mediation or insists on finding a third-party decision maker in the adversarial system, such as a judge or arbitrator, that judge or arbitrator can still order mediation.

To highlight some differences between an adversarial-style court system and mediation, compare:

Key Differences Between Adversarial Trial and Mediation		
Process Style:	Formal	Informal
Foundation on Which Decisions are Reached:	Advocacy (by you or your lawyer) Evidence Application of the law	"Interest"-based or competitive negotiation
Potential Outcomes:	Win / lose decisions or Dismissal (e.g. The court decides there is not enough evidence or no legal standards to decide your case)	Impasse or Mutual Agreement Mediator has no decision making power
Enforceability:	By power of the court	Often treated like a breach of contract
Tenor:	Adversarial advocacy: "I'm right, you're wrong, and I'll prove it."	First, listen. Then, collaborate. Finally, problem-solve.

Please note that while much of the information in this primer applies to both voluntary and court-ordered mediation, there are significant differences between the two. For example, in a court-ordered mediation, the parties may show up for the mediation, but one of the disputants may be in favor of mediating while the other may be totally opposed to it. In these types of cases, the mediator will need to assist the skeptical disputant to at least consider listening, then collaborating, and finally problem solving the dispute. By contrast, in voluntary mediation, you and your disputants enter into the process with negotiation as your common objective.

The good news is that our court system upholds mediated agreements as valid contracts, whether the mediation is voluntary or court-ordered.

Voluntary mediation also works when you and your disputant have exhausted your own ideas, or want to stop arguing and negotiate before one of you gets so frustrated you file a complaint in court.

Let's apply what has just been stated above to our two cases.

For John, communication has broken down, but not by his choice. John has not spoken with Judy about the incidents or their consequences. He knows there are issues on Judy's part. He has his own. He's determined to go forward with whatever method has the best chance of helping him reach an agreement with Judy, put the incidents behind him, and restore a neighborly relationship.

John doesn't want to wait until he's contacted by Judy's attorney or by a process server delivering Judy's complaint. These moves would signal the beginning of a formal, adversarial relationship. For his part, John seems to be the target of escalating issues with Judy's teenagers. He knows he could try to file a restraining order against the teenagers using the vandalism to his car as the basis. This too would signal the start of a formal, adversarial relationship.

Mariko knows she can move for summary possession and evict Kimo, but she wants to explore another option. She learned about mediation from an advertisement she saw in the *East Oahu Sun©*. The ad described private voluntary negotiation. She calls my number and asks for an appointment.

In Mariko's case, cost and timing of litigation are big concerns. If she decides to file a complaint, she knows she'll have to hire an attorney to prepare her complaint, conduct discovery, negotiate for her, and advocate her case in front of a judge. She is concerned an attorney will cost more than she is asking from Kimo. Mariko is juggling raising her three children with her job. She wants a predictable schedule. She also prefers a negotiating session to a court proceeding. She wants to limit exposure about her dispute with Kimo from public view. She feels voluntary mediation is the least intrusive option for resolving this dispute in the quickest and most cost-effective way.

Mediation as a "Process"

Why do people choose mediation?

Mediation is a beautifully flexible process. Mediation can be tailored to your specific case. Agreements can be flexibly written to meet your needs and those of your disputant. A mediation agreement is a contract enforceable under the law. Since you and your opponent are negotiating, the amount of "discovery" is limited. If either of you feels the negotiations are not going to get you to agreement you have the option to stop and withdraw. What happens in mediation is confidential and is protected by state law and/or the judiciary from being used in court.

Mediation is more straight-forward for most people than trial, which are characterized by formality, legal jargon, and procedures. Trials are geared towards decisions based upon the testimony and evidence that the court admits under its legal standards. One side "wins," while the other "loses." It's possible that neither of you will be satisfied with the result because neither of you can control the outcome.

Mediation is private. Normally the only written record from mediation is the agreement between the parties. Trials are public, with records of everything said, including the decision. By state law, mediation is confidential. The mediator is not subject to subpoena to testify at a subsequent hearing. Broad protections are provided to protect what took place at mediation, because in this way, you and your opponent can be more open with each other during negotiations.

Mediation is neither arbitration nor trial. It's not a gamble, with either a win or lose outcome. Neither is it a "split the baby"-type of process. Mediation is negotiation in which you and your disputant, guided by your mediator, search for and agree on solutions. Your mediator is a "vehicle" by which to focus on the issues rather than opponents focusing on each other.

Mediation works on two principle assumptions. First, mediation assumes you and your disputant are willing to negotiate. Second, mediation agreements require opponents to have authority to reach an agreement and commit to agreed upon actions. Authority issues are further described later in this primer.

In mediation, the negotiation happens through a set of collaborative activities to problem solve.

A threshold challenge in mediation is to modify opponent's views from adversarial to a willingness to listen to each other. The second challenge is to transform that willingness into problem solving. This is another area where trial and mediation are very different; unlike a judge who metes out decisions, a mediator has no decision-making power. It's up to the disputants to make all decisions, including a decision to call a stop to the mediation if it does not seem to be working. The final challenge is to draft a solution that you and your disputant have negotiated and can live with. Because neither of you has to sign onto a solution you can't accept, you are both invested in the problem-solving process.

Does the mediation process work? What are some of the reasons mediation does not work?

In many types of disputes, mediation has an enviable success rate. For example, mediation has a long history and successful track record in divorce and labor disputes. In some circumstances, however, mediation does not work at all. Mediation does not work where there is no trust or where disputants take absolute positions: "My way or no way." In one of my early neighbor-neighbor disputes there were parents and teenagers involved in a dispute with an elderly lady over a number of issues including noise. Unfortunately the teens were disrespectful of their elderly neighbor in their opening statement and even though she politely and amiably participated through three hours of negotiations the mediation failed because the disrespect shown to their elderly neighbor translated, for her, into a lack of trust they would honor their agreement.

As another example, in some disputes one of the disputants absolutely believes the other should be punished for their actions. Disputants intent on "punishing" rarely convince their opponent they should accept a punishment as part of a voluntary agreement.

Checking in with our disputants.

Let's check in with our cases, John and Mariko, and see how they are dealing with their disputes.

John is appalled by litigation. He feels the process is unnecessarily adversarial, overly intrusive and too public. He can't see himself hiring an attorney. But he's already received a call from his homeowner and medical insurers and knows he will have to fill out paperwork to justify the coverage they provide. He just can't see himself in an adversarial confrontation with Judy or her teens in front of a judge.

Mariko not only has a landlord-tenant dispute, but also has a potentially difficult work relationship issue. Mariko wants discretion. Mariko wants to understand what's going on.

Mariko would like to minimize the friction with Kimo for work reasons, but also get paid what's due under the lease.

You want to mediate. Where do you start?

Faced with a dispute and wanting to enter into private, voluntary mediation you may wish to talk to your opponent and propose mediation. Maybe, like John and Mariko, you decide to take the initiative and unilaterally approach a mediator to talk things over. You need to find a mediator. John's first step is to check out the web. Almost every mediator has a web page, such as mine at: www.mediate.com/mediatewithlh. Mariko finds her mediator through an advertisement. John follows up by asking a friend who had a dispute for a referral. If Mariko or John's cases had been very technical, they might have asked for referrals from people in their work fields. Attorneys may also know of mediators, because they may maintain lists for particular types of cases. The Yellow Pages also has "mediator" listings.

In Hawai'i, you can also find mediators within organizations, associations, schools, agencies, privately through law firms, by directly looking for mediators, or through community-based mediation centers.

In my case, I have practice mediating as a "negotiation enabler." In my style of mediation, I accept almost any type of case under the assumption that you and your opponent know your interests and subject matter best. My job is to use my skills to provide you and your opponent opportunity to collaborate and problem solve. I also do community service as a volunteer mediator at the O'ahu community-based Mediation Center of the Pacific, Inc.

If you really feel you need it, there are specialized mediators. Some are attorneys, others are retired judges, while still others come from a variety of backgrounds and life experiences.

The choice of a mediator is up to you and your opponent.

Let's look at what John and Mariko do with their cases.

John gets my name from his friend and calls me. John and I seem to strike it off over the phone, so we agree to meet for a preliminary discussion, which I call an intake.

In addition to looking at print ads, Mariko also gets some referrals from one of her attorney friends. The attorney provides names and suggests Mariko contact at least three mediators. The attorney also suggested she first contact her opponent, Kimo, to see if he's willing to enter into voluntary mediation. After thinking about it for a while, Mariko decides it would be best to contact the mediators suggested by her attorney. When she contacts me, we schedule an introductory conference.

The Initial Conference with a Mediator

What should you expect from your initial conference with a mediator? If all goes well, you should expect to:

- To be heard
- To be acknowledged
- To feel the mediator understands your case and can work with your opponent
- To get an estimate on fees for services

What do I, as mediator, expect to accomplish in an initial conference with you? I expect:

- You will understand how confidentiality works in mediation. I want you to understand, as I will also explain to your opponent, that mediation's confidentiality is broad and protective. Broadly speaking state rules protect everything that is said during mediation from use in future litigation. The intent of the confidentiality pledge is to encourage you and your disputant to be open in negotiations during mediation
- To understand your issues, interests, and needs
- To listen and to acknowledge your perspective of the circumstances of your case.
- To begin drafting a blueprint for your case. You are in my office because you need help. In many cases, it may seem the issues are overwhelmingly complex, especially when you're the one who is grappling with them. Your dispute's issues probably need some organizing. Your emotions may be high. You may

need to vent. Also, mediation may be an unfamiliar process when you come in but not when you leave.

An initial conference with a mediator is an opportunity for you and the mediator to learn whether or not mediation is appropriate for your dispute and whether, in your opinion, this mediator should mediate in your case.

As a mediator of your dispute, remember that I am not your advocate and will not take sides. I am not conducting a legal review of your case. There is a form of mediation, called evaluative mediation, that conducts legal evaluations, but it's not the process I'm explaining in this primer.

It is you and your opponent's responsibility to decide whether to retain and consult attorneys to deal with the legal issues involved in your dispute.

Our initial conference objectives are met if you leave my office satisfied you have been heard, acknowledged, understand the mediation process, have made a decision your case is suitable for mediation, and whether I am the mediator you will propose to your opponent. If you've made a decision, contact must then be made with your opponent. Before we turn to making contact, let's apply the information in this section to John and Mariko.

John wants to negotiate, collaborate and problem solve. John is non-confrontational. Remember him, ducking into his car to avoid Fluffy and the neighbors? Or, attempting to communicate with Judy after the incident, only to see her walk away crying? Plus, he also has emotions about things that have happened – why is his car dented? What about his injuries and lost workdays? He is really worried about emotions on both his, and Judy's side. He dreads going into a courtroom, a public forum. He's intimidated about testifying under oath –

not because he wants to lie, but because he's worried he'll say the wrong thing, or say something in the wrong way. He can't imagine remaining in an adversarial relationship with his neighbor. He's not sure how he will react to any testimony her teenagers will provide. The court system is not his way of resolving disputes. However regardless of the outcome of the financial issues involved, changes are needed. The tree roots are a problem. He does not want to unilaterally cut the roots at the boundary line between the properties without consultation with Judy. He doesn't want to kill the tree further escalating the situation. He's heard all kinds of stories about cases involving pets and he doesn't want Fluffy's disappearance rehashed in court. It might seem silly to some, but it would be embarrassing for John to admit he has a fear of dogs. That's his personal secret. He wants a mediator who is not only competent but also considerate of his and Judy's special concerns.

John's list of selection requirements for a mediator include:

- Listens to what he has to say
- Asks good questions
- Summarizes frequently to confirm they're on track
- Understands his issues and concerns
- Is a good "people person," who demonstrates an ability to create empathy and rapport. After all, Judy will also have to agree to mediate, and to agree to the same mediator.
- Is good at dealing with possible gender and youth issues
- Can provide some creativity to solutions
- Is reasonably priced

John summarizes the fateful events from that Monday morning to the present. He is brief and vents some of his frustrations. He tells me, as his dispute's potential mediator, what he's trying to do as well as avoid. I acknowledge his concerns. I take his story and use it to provide context for:

- Explaining the general mediation process
- Contrasting mediation with trial and arbitration
- Explaining the confidentiality of the process
- Identifying with John who needs to be involved
- Outlining preparations I will conduct with those involved
- Outlining what a mediation session might look like
- Stressing that I am not an advocate for either his or Judy's position, but a guide for their negotiation and problem solving
- Discussing potential timing
- Deciding who will be contacting each disputant

I indicate to John this is a multi-party case with a number of issues, some of which are related to each other, while others are not. My proposal will therefore have several parts, with different participants and separate mediation sessions. Preparation times for each mediation session will be included in my proposal. In addition, I explain that some of John's disputants may agree to mediation and to me as the mediator, while others may not. The disputants that do not agree will have to be handled in another way, potentially through the court system.

The next day, Mariko comes to my office. While Mariko's case is more streamlined, she is just as invested in the issues of her case and just as careful in her evaluation of me as a potential mediator. As we talk it over, we identify that the primary issue may very well be collecting back rent; however, Mariko is very concerned the dispute will have an adverse impact on her job.

Mariko seems well prepared with a clear perspective of her case and issues involved. She brings the lease, a chronology of the events, her letters to Kimo, and payment records. The apartment Kimo is renting is in a house she and her brother, Nobu, inherited from their parents. Her brother disclaimed the house, leaving Mariko as the sole owner. He helps with house maintenance and occasionally stays at the house. The rent is $1,800 per month. Based on her figures, Kimo owes her three months' back rent, plus a penalty of $150. The total is $5,500. She says she feels a bit foolish for letting the matter drag on. She thinks maybe she was naïve to let her concerns about Kimo's troubles outweigh the landlord/tenant relationship and their respective rights and responsibilities.

After listening to Mariko and acknowledging her concerns, I explain the mediation process, my role as mediator, confidentiality, and the necessary preparations, all in the context of her case. We also discuss timing, as it's very important for Mariko to schedule around her work and child care responsibilities. We further discuss her issues and needs in the context of maintaining her work relationship.

In both cases, John and Mariko decide I satisfy their requirements for a mediator, so we are able to move with them to the next step: contacting their disputants with a proposal to mediate.

Approaching Disputants About Mediating a Dispute

Remember, in this primer we're discussing voluntary mediation. Voluntary mediation means that all the disputants agree, of their own free will, to mediate the dispute. Without your opponent's agreement to mediate, and agreement on the choice of mediator, your mediation cannot occur.

We need to recognize that not all disputants are predisposed to voluntarily mediate. Statistics indicate 50% of all disputants will reject an invitation to voluntarily mediate. I'm confident that when the process of mediation is more widely known and utilized, more people will understand the benefits and be willing to mediate. We discuss these issues further, later in this document.

When you invite disputants to mediate, especially when emotions are already high, it is important not to further inflame the dispute. Unfortunately there are situations where people react negatively to the suggestion that a third party is needed to resolve the dispute. Some disputants may even take the position that there is no dispute and therefore no reason to mediate. At other times, even though you may feel there are issues, the other party considers the matter not only settled, but also closed. A clear example is a situation where a dispute has already been litigated and settled, but you consider the courts decision unfair. These kinds of cases do come up, as for example, in child custody situations pursuant to a divorce decree, but not only there.

During initial visits I work with prospective clients to help identify the most promising way to issue the invitation to mediate.

There is no magic bullet to successfully get opponents to agree to an invitation to mediate. In some cases, you and I may decide it would be best for me, the mediator, to deliver an invitation. If so:

- I introduce myself and what I do
- I identify the initiating party, the dispute, and provide the rationale for why private voluntary mediation has been proposed
- I make absolutely clear I'm not an advocate for the initiating party, nor will I be an advocate for any disputant
- I spend time with each disputant, just as I have with you, explaining mediation in the context of their potential mediation session.

If you are the one making the proposal, you and I discuss the most receptive environment in which to make an invitation and how to issue an invitation in a positive manner by communicating the central issue involved, the need for a third party, and amongst other factors, highlighting the benefits of mediation.

I also offer written materials to help the disputants to evaluate the mediation process for themselves.

If the opponent is receptive to mediating a dispute, the next step is to agree to a mediator. In John and Mariko's cases, I might be chosen, but only if their opponents also agree.

So far, we've discussed only one way to begin the voluntary mediation process – that is, you potentially contacting me as a mediator, before discussing mediation as an option with your disputant. An alternative approach is for you and your disputant to agree to voluntary mediation before contacting a mediator. In this approach, you both agree to consider several mediators before deciding which one to use. You might, for example, submit and interview mediators, separately. You and your opponent get an idea of what kind of process a specific mediator uses, and what the potential cost might be. Once you and your disputants select a mediator, you are ready to begin the mediation process.

Let's now return to John's case. When John and I discuss how to propose the mediation to Judy, John feels he should call her directly, and for me, as the mediator, to branch from there to the other disputants. He wants Judy to know he is not sitting on his hands waiting for insurers or attorneys to call him before doing something. He's also concerned about the on-going issues with her teens and he doesn't want to get to a point of confrontation. For him then, time is of the essence. Here's a sample script from his telephone call:

John's Call to Judy

John finds Judy's number, takes a deep breath, and dials.

Judy: Hello.

John: Judy, hi. This is your neighbor, John.

Judy: John, I'm not sure I want to talk to you.

John: Exactly. I'm calling about how we may be able to talk.

Judy: I'm listening.

John: First of all, I'm sorry about what happened and what is going on.

Judy: I thought you wanted to tell me how we can talk. I'm really unhappy about maybe taking this to court, and all those attorneys and adjusters, not to mention all those documents I have to sign!

John: Me, too. That's why I've contacted someone who can at least help us sort out these issues. Do you want to hear more?

Judy: Go ahead.

John: The person's a mediator and the process is called mediation. It starts by putting us in control. And mediation keeps us in control of the decision making.

Judy: Nobody can control the insurance companies and their attorneys.

John: True, but should they agree to mediation they can participate with us.

Judy: There are so many problems.

John: Exactly. The mediator has that kind of expertise -- identifying the issues, determining our interests, and helping us find ways to meet our needs. The main expertise is getting us all into the mindframe of negotiating in a collaborative way where we solve problems. I can't explain it as well as the mediator can. Maybe you can call him and at least hear what he has to say. Plus, you should check him out on your own. A mediator doesn't represent me or anybody else – it's the mediator's role just to help the negotiations. He's sort of like a professional negotiator, who can help guide our negotiations.

Judy: I'm not sold on this at all, but I'm willing to talk. What's it going to cost?

John: You can set up an intake discussion with him first, like I did. Then he'll give you an estimate. If we decide to use him, he'll draw up a proposal laying out his services and his costs. We'll split the costs.

Judy: What about privacy and confidentiality? Mrs. Murakami across the street keeps asking if we're going to sue, and Mr. Pilipo from down the block keeps asking if we're getting sued!

John: The first thing the mediator talked about was privacy and confidentiality. There are laws that protect our discussions – it's better if you talk to him about any concerns. Will you at least make the call?

Judy: All right, John I'll make the call. I can't promise anything. I'm willing to try. Let's just leave it at that. What's the guy's name and number?

* * * *

Judy and I meet. Once I get the green light to mediate, I make calls to their respective insurers. The insurers know that if the case is disputed and goes to court, they will most likely have to engage in court-ordered mediation anyway. They agree to participate.

Let's now catch up with Mariko's dispute. Mariko and I talk it over and decide that I should call Kimo.

My Call to Kimo

I send an introductory letter to Kimo. I enclose information on mediation. In the letter, I indicate I'll be calling him and request he take my phone call, if only to meet at a mutually convenient time, listing the phone number I expect to call. I give him my email address, should he wish to communicate before the call. A week passes and I make the call, only to get an "out of office" message. I ask Kimo to call me back. A few days pass and I call again.

Leo: Mr. Kimo Rapoza? Hi, my name is Leo Hura. I'm calling to ask whether you might be receptive to a voluntary negotiation with Ms. Mariko Kealoha regarding the rent and lease.
Kimo: Are you an attorney?
Leo: I have a law degree but I'm not participating as an attorney. I don't represent Ms. Kealoha, though she did ask me to call you. I'm a mediator. That means I'm a person who helps people involved in a dispute help them continue their negotiations. It's not my job to take sides. Instead, I can try to help you folks negotiate and agree on a solution to your dispute.
Kimo: I'm confused. How did you get involved?
Leo: Ms. Kealoha recognizes there may be some issues between you that must be resolved. She feels the best way is for the two of you to sit down and work on solutions, rather than go through litigation in court.
Kimo: Is that so? What's involved?
Leo: In this case, the process would be totally voluntary. It requires that you both mutually agree on all the decisions in your dispute. Voluntary mediation, the process I'm trained to help you with, is a tool. It's a tool for you folks to reach a

solution without having to go to court. The mediation process can help you folks negotiate your own solution. Part of the reason mediation works is because both you and Ms. Kealoha have a neutral person – a mediator – who steps between the two of you to help you collaborate and problem solve. Another reason mediation works is because both of you would be willing to negotiate. Negotiation is give and take. In mediation, both you and Ms. Kealoha act in your own best interests. But through the process, you may be able to find a solution that meets both your and Mariko's needs and interests. In mediation it's possible to satisfy everyone's interests and needs. Sometimes you both might have to take a little less than what you'd like. In those cases, you might agree to a solution because you've both thought about the whole situation and believe it's the best agreement you can negotiate. Either way, the decision to make the agreement belongs to each of you – both you and Ms. Kealoha would have to agree to be bound. You could disagree. If that's the case then either of you can walk away from mediation. After that, you might try to resolve your dispute through the courts or arbitration.

Kimo: Yes, but what's the cost?

Leo: The costs would be split between the two of you. I can give you a written proposal once I get a better sense of your dispute. You would have the chance to review it before accepting. I do require pre-payment before each session.

If you're at least open to the idea, maybe we should meet for a confidential intake? That way you can get a better sense of whether you're comfortable with me as a mediator. I'm a neutral party, so you can talk to me about the dispute without it getting back to Ms. Kealoha. We both know time is valuable, and I'm not going to waste yours. A meeting's important. It gives us a chance to talk about your case and answer more questions about the mediation process. Then we can assess whether I'm able to deal with your case. Again, the initial conference is confidential. Generally, if I engaged as a mediator my fees are on an hourly basis. In this case I will probably charge on a per session basis and payment is required in advance of each session. My fees are split amongst opponents. In this case you would pay half and Mariko would pay half.

Kimo: Well, let me check my schedule. Can we meet on Tuesday?

Kimo visits my office and we sit down to talk. Kimo immediately has more questions about mediation confidentiality. He asks whether certain things can be kept confidential from Mariko, if he so requests. I tell him this is an integral part of the process. I quickly give him an overview of mediation and the role of a mediator as a neutral negotiation enabler and not an advocate.

After signing a confidentiality pledge I ask Kimo for his perspective on the lease, occupancy, rent due, and offer to listen to him voice other issues he thinks may be relevant. Kimo needs to vent. Surprisingly, the venting is not about the apartment but about his relationship with his father. He expected to have a position of responsibility at his fathers firm by now. Instead, he is kept out of the operations area and assigned to projects. Several months ago, his disappointment turned to depression, followed by an ill-advised experiment with drugs. His father requires him to live on his hourly wages, so Kimo quickly ran into money trouble. Fortunately, he was able to recognize his mistake and turned to an anonymous rehab group for help. He figured he could leverage his working relationship with Mariko to buy time with the rent while he cleaned up. He continues to work. The price he paid for his façade of normalcy at work was suffering withdrawal after leaving work. Kimo says he has avoided Mariko to hide his condition. He hasn't answered her letters or calls because he is totally focused on regaining control over his life. His recovery is taking longer than he expected.

For the issue of unpaid rent, he feels it would be best if a third party were involved, especially because he's concerned about privacy. He's not sure what his position in discussions with Mariko will be. He acknowledges she could evict him. In fact he's afraid with each passing day of receiving a complaint from her lawyer. He says he knows eviction would adversely impact his recovery. I thanked him for sharing such sensitive information with me and assured him about confidentiality. However, I reminded him an exception was a threat of violence.

When Kimo leaves the office, he tells me he will agree to have me mediate his dispute. A few days later, Mariko calls to ask how the session with Kimo went. She's understandably curious why Kimo hasn't paid rent. As Kimo has requested confidentiality on this issue – at least for now – I politely re-explain to Mariko my role as a neutral and about confidentiality. Mariko recognizes that I will not violate Kimo's trust, and that she can expect the same from me in her confidences.

Having successfully engaged the opponents, we move into structuring the mediation proposal.

Mediators Provide Professional Services

Mediation, just like any profession requires skills and constant updating and periodic refreshment. Since your case is important to you, you should carefully consider and select your mediator. Part of your consideration is the skills and background of your mediator.

Each mediator brings a different skill set and can draw upon a different personal history that may help you through the mediation process.

As a mediator, I use my specific skills and unique background to draw out my clients' interests and needs. As a result, I'm able to:

- Work with disputants to embrace collaboration and problem solving
  - After attaining my undergraduate Bachelor of Science at the United States Naval Academy, I spent fourteen years on active and reserve duty; as an officer, I was responsible for managing subordinates and their issues in the days of an unpopular Vietnam War.
  - I refined these skills in a twenty-five year career as a project or business at a large multinational corporation. At Merck, I handled some of my divisions' most difficult projects and their attendant disputes, including professional disputes among engineers, disputes between areas in the company, and with vendors or suppliers. Some disputes occurred in multicultural settings: the

U.S., Sweden, France, Japan, China, Egypt, and Brazil.

o After retirement I embraced dispute resolution as a specialty. As a newly-minted attorney, I attended my first mediation training. I quickly embraced the concept of mediation – enabling people to continue negotiations – as an effective addition or alternative to our adversarial court system. Then I started turning that concept into a reality. When I moved back to Hawai'i, I plunged into mediation work with the Mediation Center of the Pacific, Inc., as well as the Association of Conflict Resolution, Hawai'i, and joined the professional organization of Mediate.com. I did extensive mediation work in district court small claims division. A hundred or more cases since, I have branched out to private practice.

I'm also able to:

- Pick up on issues, interests, and needs which are critical to the conduct of collaborative negotiations.
- I am also very comfortable in competitive negotiations. I cannot offer legal advice.
- Use my legal training to appreciate disputants' legal positions.
- Think very creatively in problem solving situations bringing forward ideas for disputants to consider
- Work with disputants from a wide variety of backgrounds, gender, different cultures, age, and differing negotiating skills
- After fourteen years of active and reserve duties in the U.S. Navy, followed by twenty-five years as a project or business team leader at private sector multinational, and picking up a law degree while working

full-time, I understand the value of time management
and self-discipline.

- Be flexible
- Grow in my experience through constant education
  and updating
- I understand
  - Technology
  - Law
  - Parenting and associated challenges for parents
  - Business relationships
  - Landlord and tenant issues

In the case of Mariko and Kimo we agreed to an hourly fee for
services.

Who is needed at each mediation session?

As obvious as the answer may seem, too many of us fail to get the right people around the negotiating table. Since mediation requires mutual agreement we need to have decision makers for each disputant represented either in person, by proxy, or within reach of the phone to review of a draft agreement.

Who is a decision maker?

In a trial, a judge is the decision maker. In a hiring situation, the hiring manager is a decision maker. In a store, the store manager is often an on-the-spot decision maker. In an insurance company, there are decision makers who can decide on behalf of the insurer to make payments. Disputes often arise among people who have no authority to make decisions to negotiate an agreement outside their limited role of being a party to a law suit. For example, a driver involved in a car accident has no authority to agree for the insurance company to make payments. The insurance contract governs. For your negotiation to be successful – that is, for it to result in an agreement between you and your disputant – the key decision makers have to be properly identified.

You, your opponent and I have to think ahead to identify decision makers who are needed to approve any potential agreement in your dispute. Also, that decision maker has to be ready to participate. If a decision maker's physical presence is not possible, we identify the best route for your draft agreement to reach a decision maker. You or your opponent can call the decision maker or you might agree on a time frame within which a decision will be reached. A time frame may be required for legal review by an attorney.

Remember, mediation is a process requiring mutual agreement between disputants who have the authority to reach a negotiated agreement.

Paperwork & Promises:
Your Fee-for-Services Agreement &
Confidentiality Pledge

If you have made it this far – made or accepted a proposal to mediate, met with and agreed upon a mediator and identified your key decision makers – you may be eager to get into a mediation session.

Before that happens, we will need to make sure some paperwork and pledges are in place. In addition to the written fee-for-services agreement, you will also need to execute a confidentiality pledge. The pledge, consistent with Hawai'i law, provides protections to you, other disputants, and me the mediator. This pledge means we can't reveal or testify about what happens at mediation in a subsequent arbitration or trial. This confidentiality pledge fosters openness during mediation. There are a few exceptions to this rule, particularly where violence is threatened or imminent against a disputant or a mediator. In general, however, the protection from introduction in a trial or at arbitration is broad.

Preparation Phase

Although negotiations in mediations often take twists and turns, preparing yourself for mediation is critical. During preparation, you and your mediator's objective is to develop a blueprint for your case. Preparation for mediation requires you and all disputants to think differently than preparation for trial or arbitration. The biggest difference is that mediation is a continuing negotiation, while trial or arbitration means advocating a position with evidence and legal principles to support a claim. In mediation, it is often unnecessary to conduct "discovery," which is the legal term for the period during which documents are legally requested and exchanged, questions asked and answered, and sworn statements taken. Instead, the mediation process allows for the informal sharing of what would be "evidence" – meaning without the legal formalities that come with a trial or arbitration. Most importantly, mediation requires you to identify issues, make statements about your interests, and agree in a way that satisfies you and your disputant's needs.

What are interest-based negotiations?

Mediations are, very often, interest-based negotiations as opposed to competitive negotiation. In interest based negotiation we work towards getting opponents to first listen to each other, decide to collaborate, and work to problem solve. In competitive negotiations opponents work to get as much as they can or to give up the least they can. Competitive negotiations work very well when there are single issues in dispute like a demand for money with little else than how much is due.

Remember our chart about issues? An issue is a source of a dispute. An issue, or source of dispute, could be John's car damaged by Judy's teenagers, Mariko's contract with Kimo where a breech has occurred, a divorce in which child custody is contested, or a budget overrun at your workplace that causes friction between accounting and research departments. In today's world issues are countless. In some disputes, there may be more than one issue.

What's an interest? Repairing John's damaged car, upholding Mariko's contract, upholding parental rights, safeguarding the budget are examples of interests. An interest is something you want to protect, further, or correct through negotiations with your disputant in order to reach agreement. For example, in the car damage case, John may be looking to get the car repaired while Judy may have an interest in avoiding the involvement of her insurance company because her insurance rates may go up.

What's a need? Money to reimburse payments made or covered, a child visitation agreement, the need to work together efficiently or peacefully, are examples of needs. Needs are the things which, if satisfied, allow us to do such things as finish business transactions and move on with life.

We are looking to identify intersections of interests among disputants. That is the meaning of "interest-based negotiations." Interests can, of course, vary among disputants.

Let's check back in with John and Judy, and then with Mariko and Kimo.

John makes it clear he is deeply concerned about relationship. He knows there are legal and monetary issues. His *interests* are to restore his and Judy's relationship and to deal with the legal and monetary issues based on negotiations between the insurers in a factual setting. His *needs* are to get a monetary settlement based on negotiations that include the insurers, stopping the vandalism and belligerent attitudes with the teenagers, deciding how to respond to the tree root invasion, deal with the disappearance of Fluffy, and to transform the relationship with Judy from, very uncomfortable to something more livable, if possible.

Judy's issues revolve around the injuries she has suffered and impact of those injuries on her work and the role she is playing as a single mother with hyperactive teenagers.

Mariko's issues concern the rent, dealing with the lease, while also dealing with any potential repercussions which may occur at the workplace. Her interests include getting Kimo to acknowledge and act on payment of the rent, deciding whether or not to renew Kimo's lease, and ensuring this dispute does not translate into a backlash at the workplace she and Kimo share. Her needs in this scenario is to get the amount due on the rent, get Kimo to explain his uncommunicative behavior and get his pledge to change, and to reach an understanding on separating what is going on in this relationship from the workplace situation.

In Mariko and Kimo's dispute, preparations become a challenge. Mariko is busy juggling family with work. Time is of the essence; she wants to get on with it. Mariko's domineering brother Nobu is increasingly pressuring her to go to court and evict Kimo. He's especially angry at Kimo for being there having not paid his rent for over three months. In separate sessions Mariko and I work on this concern. Mariko decides she wants me to ask Kimo for a payment for the current month. She also decides to put a time frame on collecting more money.

Kimo, meanwhile wavers between hope and despair, trying to develop a position he can support. In one session he drops into despair when I bring up payment for the current month's rent. I help Kimo frame his alternatives by asking him whether he knows what a judge at summary possession will do. He says no, but that he has a friend who is an attorney and could find out. The next day, Kimo comes in with a check for $1,800 he managed to borrow from a friend.

The Mediator's Role During Preparation

Not all mediators utilize a preparatory period for mediation. I find it very useful to focus you and your disputant on your issues, interests, and needs. This may sound simple, but disputants who are inexperienced with negotiation may get stalled by reading their list of grievances, reciting demands, and venting. While skilled mediators should be good listeners, it's an important part of my job to empower you to resolve issues. Going through preparation is key to shifting gears to the next step – interest-based negotiations – and toward a successfully negotiated agreement.

That's why I work hard to help you concentrate on your issues, interest, and needs. Generally, I do this by helping you and your disputants prepare opening statements for a joint session attended by both of you. A good opening statement sets the stage for mediation. Recrimination or accusations are generally not very conducive to meaningful negotiations. A helpful way to focus your opening statement is to answer the following two questions: "Why am I voluntarily mediating?" and "What do I hope to accomplish?"

For example after discussion with John he decides his opening statement will be:

"I want to work with Judy and the other disputants on issues which arose that fateful Monday morning when Judy and I were injured. I'm here to work on the issues of medical bills we both have. I'm also here to work on issues about how we plan to interact as neighbors when these problems are resolved. I hope we can work together collaboratively to solve each problem."

Similarly, Judy comes up with:

"It's really unfortunate we had these incidents. I need to work with John on resolving a number of issues. I'm overwhelmed by the problems as the result of my broken leg. I have issues with who pays what. I'm still looking for my dog. As a single mother, it was hard enough to take care of teenagers when I was healthy. I'm even more challenged than I was before. Let's see if we can work collaboratively to solve each problem."

A few days later, Mariko gets ready:

"I leased an apartment to Kimo. The nonpayment of rent over the last three months is bad enough but it occurred without explanation or communication on payment. In the meantime, I've been paying for utilities, taxes, and other expenses used by Kimo. I hope we can work out payment and Kimo's tenancy."

Kimo also prepares his opening statement:

"I've been unable to pay the rent and realize this creates a situation in which I can be evicted. However, I hope we can collaborate on a payment plan and resolve any other issues associated with my remaining at the apartment."

Notice that, despite some deep seated emotions, John, Judy, Mariko and Kimo have taken care to avoid inflammatory language or make a personal attack. As in every encounter, first impressions can have a marked impact. Your opening statement can shape how your mediation develops and ends.

Notice also that in their opening fixed positions are not taken. Judy could have said, "I want John to find Fluffy by next week or pay for her value, including the loss of her love and affection," but she focuses on her issues instead. She does well, because setting terms for an agreement too early in the mediation may make it more difficult to negotiate. What if John has an equally acceptable, but different suggestion? Or Judy hears what John has to say, and realizes he has issues she can help problem solve? By taking a position in her opening statement, Judy would have closed the door on this possibility, and John might have become defensive, entrenching himself in his positions. The more open minded you and your disputants can be during the mediation, the easier it will be for you to work through the process. Your opening statement sets the stage.

Opening (Joint) Session

After preparations have been completed, the day comes for your joint mediation session. You and your opponents, by yourselves, with your attorneys or perhaps as represented by your attorneys, may gather at the mediation site for a "joint session." If you and your disputants cannot sit in the same room, you may alternatively sit in separate rooms and your mediator will shuttle between you in separate sessions called "caucuses."

Together or separately, your mediator explains to you and your opponents the process, "confidentiality," and asks everyone involved to sign the "confidentiality pledge" agreeing to the principle "what's said in the mediation room stays in the room," and that the pledges are legally binding. So far in Hawai'i, the courts have protected the confidentiality of mediation proceedings.

Your mediator will also explain the ground rules. Ground rules in mediation are designed to keep peace between you and your disputant during the mediation, maintain the dignity of everyone involved, and to help you work within boundaries to keep you focused on issues, interests, and needs, and not, for example, on the other disputants. Civility is a goal. If you or your opponent focus on each other, or the mediator, negotiations will stall or fail. Use of offensive language – four-letter words or name calling – quickly raises emotions. That's why their use is usually prohibited by the ground rules. The purpose of your mediation is to grapple with the issues, but this purpose can be quickly forgotten if you or your disputant feel you are not respected by the other side. Other ground rules might cover a time limits – on occasion, the maximum time is set for a session. When your mediator goes over these and all the other ground rules for your session, you and all the participants are asked to agree to them. That way, if ground rules are broken, the mediator can intercede and remind the disputant about the agreement to abide by them. If the behavior continues or further deteriorates, the mediator may ask the disputants to physically separate into different rooms or even halt the mediation.

At the initial session, you and your disputant make your opening statements without interruption. With an opening statement properly prepared, it is brief, expresses your issues, and emphasizes your purpose for mediating. If your opponent has a question about something you've said, they will write the question down and ask it after your opening statement, consistent with the ground rules.

Your disputant gets a chance to make an opening statement following the same ground rules.

Your mediator will then help you move to the next step. Your mediator may take a few moments to acknowledge your opening statements to help you establish a listening environment with your opponent.

One way that I respond to these opening statements is to consolidate what each of you has communicated into a common problem statement.

After John and Judy make their opening statements, I say:

"Thank you both for indicating a willingness to work collaboratively and problem solve. You both have indicated there are issues that require some scrutiny of the past and some reconciliation in the present. Issues that stem from past events mean both of you have insurance issues to negotiate between yourselves and your insurers. There may be questions of fault. There are issues in the present. For example, there are behavioral issues in communicating as neighbors. And there are future issues, as you both indicated you intend to remain in the neighborhood where Judy, you will continue to raise your teenagers, and John, you want peace."

My objective is to solidify a collaborative and problem-solving environment, which John and Judy indicated they wish to have. We'll return to John and Judy in the section, "Narrowing the Issues: Transitioning from Past to Present and Future."

An unexpected turn in Mariko and Kimo's dispute:

On the day of Mariko and Kimo's mediation, they both arrive and appear nervous. Mariko has brought her brother, Nobu, who immediately gives Kimo stink eye. Kimo seems startled, but quickly covers. As I was unprepared for Nobu's participation, I ask for some separate time with each of the parties, starting with Mariko. The parties agree. It is tense moment.

Unexpected participants are not uncommon occurrences. At times opponents will refuse to sit in the same room with exclamations like "What's she doing here?" For purposes of example we assume we let Nobu stay. In our separate caucus, Mariko tells me she has come to her senses and realizes she needs more support in the mediation session. Mariko says, "Nobu has a better business sense. He isn't burdened with the work relationship between myself and Kimo and I trust Nobu's judgment."

Kimo, on the other hand, tells me he's upset. Not because he feels threatened by Nobu, but because Kimo wants privacy. He feels Nobu's presence is more likely to compromise his privacy. With privacy as his main concern, I ask Kimo if he would approve Nobu's presence if Nobu agrees to the confidentiality pledge. Kimo gives a short nod.

When we regroup, we review confidentiality, this time drafting an agreement that Nobu will not discuss what happens at the mediation sessions in which he participates. After some discussion back and forth an agreement is reached and everyone signs the agreement. Had Kimo refused to agree to Nobu's presence the mediator would have to work with Mariko and Nobu to work out whether they were agreeable to the exclusion.

We move to opening statements. Mariko opens. Mariko's initial opening statement has changed. Now she has taken a position, demanding back rent, and requesting that Kimo move out within the notice period. It seems she has partially adopted her brother's position.

Kimo opens with an apology for not having paid the rent and indicates he is willing to pay. He says he hopes to negotiate an extension to the lease for an additional six month.

Nobu stands up and says, "No way!"

Kimo's face flushes with anger, but he holds himself in check. Mariko remains stoic.

As mediator I restate as follows:

"Mariko, you are here because back rent plus penalties are due and in addition you seek to end the tenancy. You need a total of $5,500. You also need Kimo's agreement to vacate the apartment by the end of next month, which is within the notice period. Kimo, you are here because you agree you owe the $5,500 and you need to work out an agreement for repayment. In addition, you want to extend the lease for an additional period of six months." I pause for nods of acknowledgment. "You're both here to work out an agreement on payment of the rent, and we need to work on the issue which still separates you, vacating or extending the lease."

Nobu jumps in, "Kimo, you have to go."

This time, Kimo responds in anger with two words, one of which is an expletive. Before things go any further, I intervene and remind Nobu and Kimo of the ground rules and their agreement to abide by them. Mariko remains silent.

I decide it is time to go into separate sessions with each disputant.

Separate Sessions – "Caucus"

Are disputants required to be in the same room?

No. Sometimes, it is inappropriate to have disputants in the same room at the same time. Often, separate sessions are called for when you or your opponent do not want to share sensitive information. At the same time, this information may be critical to move the negotiation forward. In that case, you or your opponent may move to separate sessions with your mediator. Separate caucuses are often used when emotions are running too high or there are safety concerns in placing the parties in the same room. When safety concerns do arise it is not uncommon to conduct a mediation using only separate caucuses.

Joint sessions often work well. Joint sessions offer advantages in economy of time, the ability for you to observe and for opponents to read body language and hear directly what is said and the way it is said. It also gives you the ability to respond in the presence of, if not directly to, your opponent through the mediator.

However, in a caucus, you and the mediator retreat into an individualized session to further explore or refocus your issues, interests, and needs in light of any opening statements or at various points in the mediation process. Your mediator will at all times honor you or your opponent's requests to withhold specific information from the other party. We discussed this above but it's worth repeating in the context of the caucus.

Mediator Intercessions

Generally, but particularly in caucuses, your mediator may "intercede." This means your mediator will use verbal techniques – summarizing, reframing, reflecting back to you, or doing a "reality check" – to help you find common ground with your disputant. These techniques would take significant space to address and explain so it will have to suffice to offer a few examples in this primer. An intercession provides an opportunity for you or your opponent to better explain or understand each other. Try not to be offended if your mediator intercedes in the discussion with questions like: "Have you thought about ...?" or "Is it in your best interest to ...?" or does a "reality check." A popular reality check is, "what do you think a judge would decide in these types of circumstances?" The purpose of intercessions is to help you think through the issues, sometimes in ways you might not have considered.

Mediation is not a Trial

Also remember, you don't have to convince any mediator you are in the right, like you would before a judge who bases her decision on the evidence and how it fits into the framework of the law. Rather, a mediator needs to understand your perspective on issues and how it fits into the framework of your negotiating position. It is not in your, or your opponent's, interest to lie. If your opponent hears, or the mediator conveys for you, information which is a lie, this can easily destroy trust. Most experienced mediators share a good degree of skepticism about "absolute facts."

In separate sessions, the mediator normally asks whether anything you have said should remain confidential from the other disputant, and will honor that. Why would you want to withhold from your disputant, but tell the mediator? Confidentiality allows you to share information with the mediator that articulates "the why" behind something, but that a disputant just does not need to know in the course of negotiation. For example, a party may have a terminal illness requiring expedited negotiations. This explains why they are negotiating with urgency but they still want the illness information withheld. The mediator is obliged to withhold this information even if the disputant asks, "What's the hurry"? Confidential information exchanges between disputant and mediator are common.

Returning to Mariko and Kimo's mediation, my first caucus is with Mariko and Nobu. Mariko starts by explaining Nobu and Kimo knew each other when Nobu was a sophomore and Kimo was a senior in high school. Apparently, they had a fight over a girl and "talk" continued for some years afterwards until they lost contact. Has some of that emotion come back with involvement in this mediation? Nobu does not agree that the past has anything to do with the present: "I just don't see why my sister should allow Kimo to stay in the apartment, that's all." Mariko says, "It was such a long time ago. I don't think it is important." I acknowledge their statement to that effect and reiterate a need to focus on the issues and not one another. I ask them whether they'd like to like some private time to discuss their respective positions before we continue. They nod. We break. When I return, Mariko and Nobu agree there will be no further outbursts. Mariko will do the talking. We discuss body language. Nobu says he will maintain his composure. They ask that I simply acknowledge to Kimo I am aware of their past confrontation without getting into details. I agree.

I then meet with Kimo, who is upset. I decide to listen. Kimo's initial position was to agree to pay Mariko the rent he owed, plus penalties; however, he wanted to extend his lease for another six months. He felt the upcoming project was his big chance to prove to his father he could get things done. With his recovery still in progress, he did not want to introduce another complication – finding a new place and moving. This was going to be a challenging mediation.

I simply convey Mariko and Kimo's assurances of keeping the proceedings civil, which is enough for Kimo to return to the table. On the way back to a joint session, Kimo says, "I'm sure they told you about the girl in high school, but let me tell you – he should be happy I saved him from that one." I simply nod acknowledgment. You probably noticed I chose not to bring up the subject of the fight. In addition to honoring requests to keep information confidential from their opponents mediators do not necessarily use all information they are given freedom to convey to the other side in separate caucuses. In this case, Kimo wanted to re-focus and to keep the negotiations going. And, in this case he did offer an acknowledgment about the incident and there wasn't a need to dwell on the fight as an issue.

We return to joint session.

Narrowing the Issues: Transitioning from Past to Present and Future

In just about every mediation, the past, to some degree, provides a "history," background, or context. However, for negotiations to proceed to problem solving, your mediator endeavors to move you and your disputant's interests and needs to the future. Questions that may help you move to the future include:

- Where do we go from here?
- What is the future going to look like?
- How are we going to get there?

The mediation process is often incremental, with small steps taken, for the disputants to be able to reach a "common problem statement." Let's examine a damaged car situation:

Opening Statement:

Anthony: My car's been damaged. Repairs are estimated at $6,000.00. Since the damage is not covered by insurance, I'm here to negotiate a settlement.

Trevor: I'm here to discuss the event and damage to your car. Although I acknowledge I threw the shot-put, I am here to negotiate a reasonable settlement only for the damages caused by the shot-put.

After the opening statement and throughout the process a mediator is looking for "common ground" around which to build a tangible solution to the opponent's dispute. When I find common ground, a technique I use is to construct a "common problem-statement" as a way of communicating with opponents what I see as a potential common and achievable objective for a negotiated solution. An example follows:

"Anthony's car was damaged. Trevor you acknowledge your shot-put hit Anthony's car. Through this mediation both of you have a need to settle on an amount to cover the damages, if possible."

In this case, where there is only one issue – the amount of the settlement – structuring a problem statement is fairly straight-forward. I can help focus Anthony and Trevor into a achieving a common monetary range, and from there, to agreement.

Whether or not you have a common problem statement, your negotiations can begin to move towards the identification of options and alternatives. An "option" is a potential solution that requires further study, while an "alternative" is already a potential choice. Some of the options and alternatives you identify during mediation may eventually form your mutual agreement.

You and your disputant may presuppose there is only one answer to a problem (and you may disagree about what that one answer is). In mediation, mutual agreement is your goal. If each of you realizes there are multiple potential answers to your dispute, your positions may soften and you can then achieve a negotiated solution.

Mediation looks for answers to problems by identifying more than one potential solution. Since there are at least two disputants in a dispute, there are usually at least two altern-atives, commonly very divergent. Another beauty of mediation is the search for, consideration, and use of alternatives developed in the process of negotiation.

Let's take a look at how this develops in our two cases.

Considering Alternatives and Options to Reach an Agreement

When parties in a dispute turn from opponents, into collaborators, looking to solve problems, the path forward is often developed in joint session. We have such a situation in John and Judy's case. John and Judy have agreed to work together to sort out the bills and costs with their insurers. They agree on a plan which will allow Judy to reign in the teen's behavior towards John and make amends for the damage caused to his car. They believe they can get the insurers to buy into their plan. The mediator's role in such a situation is to work with the parties to crystallize the elements of their collaborative efforts into an Agreement. We'll talk about the Agreement later. Poor Fluffy has not been mentioned. What is the reason behind this breakthrough? In this case Judy and John needed an ice breaker to what was, for both, a shocking experience, creating an awkward situation for direct communications. They needed a forum in which they could gingerly feel their way out of a bad situation.

Unfortunately the situation with Mariko and Kimo does not go as smoothly.

Impasse

No discussion on mediation is complete without a discussion of "impasse." Impasse, in the context of mediation, translates to "no agreement." Since no one involved in the mediation has the power to force anyone else to agree, impasse is always possible. Impasse can occur if you and/or your opponent:

- hold onto fixed positions
- cannot overcome strong emotions
- cannot trust the other person
- believe a decision at trial provides greater enforceability
- feel that "I just want the court to make the decision."

When Mariko, Nobu, and Kimo return to the joint session, I suggest we work on the rent issue first. They agree and we quickly move through each party's proposals. We manage to agree on a payment plan, with $900 today followed by payments of $900 each month until the full amount is repaid. The last payment will be slightly larger to close out the repayments.

We then turn to the issue of tenancy. There is significant back and forth trying to reach common ground but we fail to find an agreement. After several hours, and considering numerous alternatives, Mariko finally says, "I guess I'll have to file for summary possession." Kimo, exhausted, just says, "Do what you have to do." He walks out. Mariko, visibly upset, thanks me. She and Nobu leave. This is an impasse, and some mediations end this way.

Reaching and Documenting Agreement

The desired outcome of your mediation session is an agreement. Mediation offers you and your disputant a lot of flexibility to tailor your agreement for your mutual needs. An agreement can be a single sentence, or it can be volumes long. Agreements can be temporary ("interim") or final. If your dispute has a lot of issues you may develop a number of agreements to resolve your issues from separately scheduled mediation sessions. If your agreement requires legal review, that must be arranged and executed by you and/or your opponents attorneys. In the type of mediation we discussed above your mediator does not give legal advice. Since many mediators are not attorneys they cannot offer legal advice because it would potentially constitute the unauthorized practice of law.

An example of a simple agreement between Anthony and Trevor in our car accident case:

1. Trevor agrees to pay Anthony $3,000 to settle Anthony's claim for damages.
2. Anthony agrees to accept Trevor's payment to settle all claims for the damages, which occurred on April 1 if Trevor pays by September 1.

If the damages had been covered by Trevor's insurance, the agreement could have expressly referred to an insurance damage claim estimate, car repair estimates, or police report, as appropriate. If a complaint had been filed in court, the case number would be included.

In more complex cases, the need for legal review by attorneys would be much greater and can very easily include additional documentation, for example contracts, to fulfill the intent and agreed upon resolution reached in mediation.

Remember that an agreement is an enforceable contract. If it is breached, you or your opponent can take action in a court.

Once you and your opponent have created your agreement, you need to sign it. All the opponents will get copies, and one will be kept by your mediator.

Let's get back to John and Judy's dispute. Remember that John and Judy reached an interim agreement to hold separate mediations based on their issues list. They had agreed to and documented a plan, including a schedule. The schedule is part of their agreement.

Over several sessions, they resolve each issue. Their insurance companies come to an agreement on liability and costs. They hire an arborist to treat the tree and split the costs. They come to an agreement they can both live with to deal with the teenagers. John and Judy decide they don't want to talk about Fluffy. They shake hands and leave.

Let's also check in with Mariko and Kimo.

The day after Kimo storms out of the session, I make follow-up calls. Mariko and Kimo know I'm available if they change their minds. Kimo calls and says he wants to return. Mariko also agrees to return, and without Nobu. In our session, Kimo explains there are things going on in his life that make it important for him to stay where he is. Mariko reconsiders her position after realizing staying was so important to Kimo. We prepare an agreement covering the repayment plan. Mariko gets a check for $900. The agreement indicates that if all other conditions remain the same, and if Kimo makes the next payment plus the overdue rent, his lease will be extended for an additional six months. We set deadlines for the overdue payments.

They sign the agreement, shake hands and leave my office with their copies. On the way out, I overhear them talking about their upcoming project together. I file my copy of their agreement, and shred my notes.

Conclusion

Negotiation has a very long history. Mediation, where a third party intercedes or steps into the dispute, also has a long history. A merger and integration of the two is now entering into mainstream American justice. Today, skilled mediators offer disputants a real alternative to courts or arbitration. Mediation has many applications. We have highlighted a number of them but the application of mediation has been successfully used even in disputes between nations. In sharing the information provided in this primer, I hope you will find it easier to select and agree with your opponent to voluntarily mediate. If not, you may still find yourself mediating in a court-ordered mediation. Either way, I encourage you to take mediation seriously. It's an opportunity for you and your opponent to maintain control over your dispute, from the moment you agree to mediate, select your mediator, and tailor your agreement to your needs. Understanding the process is critical. Mahalo for working through this primer.

Epilogue

John works with a specialist in phobias to overcome his fear of dogs. Eventually, he gets to the point where he contemplates buying a dog – the closest match to Fluffy, in fact. By chance he knows a vet on the other side of the island, a friend of a friend, to whom he goes for information on breeders. The vet says, "I just admitted the kind of dog you're looking for." When John approaches the kennel, a German Shepherd emits an unmistakable bark: Fluffy's. When John shows up at Judy's front steps, the reunion between Judy and Fluffy is beyond joyous. As John starts to walk away he feels this tap on his shoulder and when he turns he gets a hug from Judy. The rest is history. Today, John and Judy live in the same house and rent the other. But unfortunately they have a tenant "from hell." They believe they know what they need to do; they've incorporated dispute resolution into the lease, starting with mandatory mediation. The teens are off to college. I haven't heard from Mariko or Kimo although I heard a rumor Nobu had been arrested for assault and battery in a silly dispute. With whom I do not know. Life goes on. Peace.

Appendix 1
Mediation Mini - Primer

Mediation is:
- ➤ Communications Process
- ➤ Focused on furthering negotiations to reach mutual agreement
- ➤ Using a third party intercessor called a mediator

Example of Issues to which Mediation Applies:
- ➤ Money – price, damages
- ➤ Broken promises – contract, child custody
- ➤ Court ordered – focused on the issues in the litigation
- ➤ Neighbor with neighbor

One Basic Mediation Process:
- ➤ Mutual agreement to mediate and mediator to be used
- ➤ Preparation for the mediation by mediator with each side
- ➤ Mediation Session(s)
    - ▪ Joint
    - ▪ Separately, with mediator shuttling between sides
    - ▪ Agreeing on a common problem statement
        - ❖ Party A's problem is … to resolve, needs …
        - ❖ Party B's problem is … to resolve, needs …
    - ▪ Get to within negotiating range or identify alternatives
    - ▪ Find common ground
    - ▪ Close gaps or select alternatives to consider
    - ▪ Unable to work out differences identify Best Alternative to a Negotiated Agreement (BATNA)
    - ▪ Resolve and write agreement

Key Features:
➢ Mutual agreement required during entire process-
   exception: stop
➢ Confidentiality (check state rules)

Fees
➢ Relatively small cost for preparation followed by a flat fee
   proposal, costs split
➢ Hourly
➢ Combination of two

Appendix 2
References

Booher, Dianna, *"Communicate with Confidence"*, McGraw Hill, Inc. 1994

Finalayson, Andrew, *"Questions That Work"*, AMACOM, 2001

Hamlin, Sony, *"How to Talk so People Listen"*, HarperCollins Publishers, 2006

Moore, Christopher, *"The Mediation Process"*, JosseyBass, 2003

Wiggins, Charles B., *"Negotiation and Settlement Advocacy"*, Thomson/West, 2005

About the Author

Leo and wife Marika live in Hawaii where Leo practices mediation. Leo worked as a business team leader and project manager at Merck & Co. for 25 years. Leo's education includes BS from USNA, JD from Seton Hall University Law School, and a graduate business certificate from Wharton. Leo has been developing his passion and expertise in mediation since 2000. In his practice he deals with business with business, business with client, and interpersonal issues requiring a third party to intercede in failing negotiation. Leo loves to write. He uses creative nonfiction to reach potential clients considering mediation. This primer for mediation utilizes a storyline where Leo "talks story" while developing a clients understanding about and benefits to be derived from voluntary mediation.

Leo Hura – JD, Mediator
Mediate with LH, LLC
www.mediate.com/mediatewithlh